SLIP STREAM

HOW TO SPEND A
BILLION

ANNE ROONEY

EDGE FRANKLIN WATTS

LONDON • SYDNEY

First published in 2013 by
Franklin Watts
338 Euston Road
London NW1 3BH

Franklin Watts Australia
Level 17/207 Kent Street
Sydney NSW 2000

© Franklin Watts 2013

(ebook) ISBN: 978 1 4451 2907 5
(hb) ISBN: 978 1 4451 1955 7
(library ebook) ISBN: 978 1 4451 2588 6

Dewey Classification number: 428.6

A CIP catalogue record for this book is
available from the British Library.

Series Editors: Adrian Cole and Jackie Hamley
Series Advisors: Diana Bentley and Dee Reid
Series Designer: Peter Scoulding
Picture researcher: Diana Morris

Printed in China

Franklin Watts is a division of
Hachette Children's Books,
an Hachette UK company.
www.hachette.co.uk

Acknowledgements:
Rostislav Ageev/Shutterstock: 17c.
Blue Orange Studio/Shutterstock: 14.
ChameleonsEye/Shutterstock: 11.
df028/Shutterstock: 10.
Emmanuel Dunand/AFP/Getty Images: 8-9.
Mark Eaton/Dreamstime: 21.
Greg Balfour Evans/Alamy: front cover, 7.
www.hammacher.com <http://www.
hammacher.com <http://www.hammacher.
com> > : 16.
Iakov Kalinin/Shutterstock: 15.
Mandalay Bay, Las Vegas: 4.
Natursports/Shutterstock: 18.
Nazdezhda1906/Dreamstime: 12.
1001nights/istockphoto: 17b.
Jose Antonio Perez/Shutterstock: 22.
courtesy Serendipity 3: 5.
Thorpe Park: 6.
TWPhoto/Corbis: 13.
Edwin Verin/Dreamstime: 20.
worldswildlifewonders/Shutterstock: 23.
Yanniskourt/Dreamstime: 19.
Rashevskyi Viacheslav/Shutterstock: 1.

Every attempt has been made to clear
copyright. Should there be any
inadvertent omission please apply to the
publisher for rectification.

CONTENTS

YOUR BILLION DOLLAR WIN!

What would you buy with one billion dollars ($1,000,000,000)?

Fancy a snack?

Buy one of the world's best burgers (no chips)!

$5,000

Would you like ice cream, too? Why not try vanilla, with chocolate, cherries, caviar (fish eggs) and gold.

$1,000

Spent: $6,000   Remaining: $999,994,000.

FUN WITH FRIENDS

Hurtle upside-down at
90 kilometres per hour.
Is that your idea of fun?

Build your own rollercoaster.
You could scream all the way!

$31,000,000

Spent: $31,006,000   Remaining: $968,994,000.

SMART WHEELS

You need to get around. This carbon fibre bike from Japan is great.

$200,000

Spent: $31,206,000 Remaining: $968,794,000.

GET A PET

How about a panda? Just one would be lonely, so get two.

Panda pen: **$387,500**
Panda-rent to China: **$992,000** a year
Bamboo: **$108,500** a year

Total
$1,488,000

Spent: $32,694,000 Remaining: $967,306,000.

GO SWIMMING

Time for a swim? An infinity pool seems to go on forever. It looks as if you can swim off the edge of the world!

$300,000

(You can't afford an indoor beach. That costs two billion.)

Spent: $32,994,000   Remaining: $967,006,000.

YOUR OWN ISLAND

If you really want a beach,
then buy your own island.
Make sure it is somewhere warm!

$2,000,000

Spent: $34,994,000   Remaining: $965,006,000.

EXPLORE THE SEA

Use a personal submarine round your island.
This one looks like a killer whale. You need a
boat to use it with.

Submarine: **$100,000**
Pirate ship: **$2,500,000**
Crew: **$620,000** a year

Total:
$3, 220,000

Spent: **$38,214,000** Remaining: **$961,786,000.**

TIME FOR SPORTS

Buy Cristiano Ronaldo to play for your school football team. Your team will never lose again!

$124,000,000 transfer fee
$16,000,000 a year

Total
$140,000,000

Spent: $178,214,000 Remaining: $821,786,000.

DRESS UP!

Learn to be a space traveller in a real astronaut suit.

$9,000,000

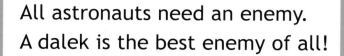

All astronauts need an enemy.
A dalek is the best enemy of all!

$5,000

Total
$9,005,000

Spent: $187,219,000 Remaining: $812,781,000.

FLY TO THE MOON

Now you have the suit — use it! Book a seat on the first tourist trip to the Moon.

$750,000,000

You still have $62,781,000! What will you buy?

INDEX

FOR TEACHERS

About

Slipstream is a series of expertly levelled books designed for pupils who are struggling with reading. Its unique three-strand approach through fiction, graphic fiction and non-fiction gives pupils a rich reading experience that will accelerate their progress and close the reading gap.

At the heart of every Slipstream non-fiction book is exciting information. Easily accessible words and phrases ensure that pupils both decode and comprehend, and the topics really engage older struggling readers.

Whether you're using Slipstream Level 1 for Guided Reading or as an independent read, here are some suggestions:

1. Make each reading session successful. Talk about the text before the pupil starts reading. Introduce any unfamiliar vocabulary.

2. Encourage the pupil to talk about the book using a range of open questions. For example, what do they think would be the best way to spend a billion dollars?

3. Discuss the differences between reading non-fiction, fiction and graphic fiction. What do they prefer?

For guidance, SLIPSTREAM Level 1 – How to Spend a Billion has been approximately measured to:

National Curriculum Level: 2c	ATOS: 2.0*
Reading Age: 7.0–7.6	Guided Reading Level: H
Book Band: Turquoise	Lexile® Measure (confirmed): 410L

*Please check actual Accelerated Reader™ book level and quiz availability at www.arbookfind.co.uk

Slipstream Level photocopiable **WORKBOOK 2** ISBN: 978 1 4451 1798 0 available – download free sample worksheets from: www.franklinwatts.co.uk